The Essence of
My Soul

Clianda Florence

Book Coach – Robin Devonish
Cover Design – Alanna Nelson
Editing and Layout – Pen Publish Profit™
Interior Design – www.queekpub.com

ISBN 13: 979-8-9864269-0-7
LCCN: 2022916239
Printed in the United States of America

ACKNOWLEDGMENTS

To Robin Devonish and CaTyra Polland, I want to thank both you Sis-Stars for your hard work and guidance throughout this amazing journey.

Thank you my beautiful, talented, artistic cousin Alanna Nelson for your artistic design.

To my friends and family that listened and critiqued my work along the way I thank you.

To my dear friend and mentor Sis. Dicker you always told me to tell my story and put it on paper. I didn't believe I had much to say, but now I have the Strength 2 Say what's on my heart. Thank you for watching over me in heaven.

DEDICATION

To the one who brought joy inside my tears, you made me complete and restored me at my broken places!

CONTENTS

BECOMING

When you think of **Love** it's something rare, beautiful, painful, growth, giving, sharing, and becoming someone that is full of so much potential.

As I began this journey pouring myself out on paper like a drink offering, I witnessed another side of myself became awakened; I began to pour into me holistically.

Often times when becoming mothers, professionals, and wives' something happens.
The needs of others become the focal point and often our dreams, projects and goals take a back seat, or we will say to ourselves "I'll get right back to that!" Before we realize it , ten years has passed and we **Become** engulfed with other things and consumed by our various roles.

I was a victim of that!

I believe other men and women can attest to the very same narrative.

When we put "Self" on the shelf, we lose touch with who we are and our creative genius.
It is in that moment you must brush yourself off and say, "NO MORE!" I AM MORE!!!!!
We must remind ourselves we are more than what we

are, what our children, spouse, boss or others perceive us to be; I would even say ourselves.

Don't be afraid to Step Out on Faith and *Become* who you have wanted to be.

Take out that business plan you worked on years ago. The hobby that everyone has shared should be turned into a business, the step that your boss has been pushing you to take, do it!
The book you've been meaning to write but could not find the time.
The love you wanted to give or the relationship you need to let go.

Become what God has destined you to BE.

Remember, it's a process.
Be patient with yourself and knowing you must surround yourself with a
Fan Crew and not *Flame Throwers*.
Position yourself within a *Crew* that encourages you, is honest and will ride the wave with you.
Remove anyone that will be jealous and tell you that you are dreaming too big or you're too ambitious.
Become the version of you that has been screaming within.

Soar like an eagle and investigate the sun.

Ask God for direction and discernment.

Know it's a journey not a fixed destination.

Allow yourself to travel down hidden paths.
Don't be discouraged when you get off track.
Remember, it's fine to give yourself space to create new ones.

For its not the journey alone, but who and what you ***Become*** along the way!

IT HAPPENED

He and I are so different, come from opposite sides of the tracks, but sometimes it just happens like that.

He has Southern Swag, dresses nice, like my father you smell him before he walks into a room. He commands attention without opening his mouth.
It happened one day this **New York Woman** and this **Southern Man** hooked up and he led me by the hand.
He took me on a mental trip, causing me to think of "Westside Story" type of Love Shit!

We are similar in so many ways, yet different.
We gaze into each other's eyes with the "It Happened" stare.
Not having a care in the world, we bring the best out of one another and can't walk away.

It happened in an organic way.
The Love is mutual, everyone can see causing them to stop and stare.

Like Love Jones "he is the blues in my left thigh, trying to become the funk in my right."

This really is **Love!** Not too often do you experience the raw purity of a love like this.
Our situation happened in such a natural way, watching

each other like prey, a moth to a flame burned by the fire in my Janet Jackson voice, that's the way Love goes!
Like the movie Brown Sugar, I make our love story mix tape.
Keith Sweat "Make it Last Forever" came to mind when he hit me with "your irrevocable in my life, we are the perfect fit."

What can I say he got me open dancing in the rain, making me want to tattoo.

"It Happened" on my hand, across my hip, and on my heart. He's got a hold on me, and I of him.

Will these feeling continue to happen?
Will our love story weather life storms?
Shit happens, anything could go wrong!

This right here happens to be something different and strong.
The Power Couple making moves, changing the game; bossing up love & respect, hittin em with a new name.

Love is something so fragile and pure.

He takes my breath away, makes me feel like I'm in high school again.
He's my crush, the star quarterback and I'm in the stands screaming his name for the win.
Yes, it happened, his hands, my thighs, he went up high kissed me slow I had nowhere to go except in his arms where I'm covered not afraid to be me.

THAT'S THE WAY

As I sit, I wonder what was it about me that caught his eye, that pushed him to put his hat in the ring to give Love a try?

The Jones has fallen on us both all we see are one another. One day he reached out to me with the most beautiful poem by one of my favorite poets Langston Hughes, "To Artina"

"I will take your heart
I will take your soul out of your body
As though I were God
I will not be satisfied
With the touch of your hand
Nor the sweet of your lips alone.
I will take your heart for mine.
I will take your Soul.
I will be God when it comes to you!"

I was speechless because those words are both bold and deep.
The way he desires to take care of me the way God does speaks to the essence of the man he is when it comes to me.

I find it romantic in these days and times that a man seeks to take care of me in such a way.
This man moves me like a Smooth Jazz song.

ORGANIC GROWTH

What has been ordained and orchestrated doesn't require hard work to grow, it just grows naturally.

The beautiful thing about us is ***true love*** is like changing of seasons.
No matter what you do or desire nothing can stop the transition.

The leaves will fall, and grass will flourish, we have placed ourselves in something that will indeed keep on growing.

Know that it's natural to fear, become anxious or try and resist.
When love is pure it moves fluently like water from the falls.

You have the task of managing something that you can't control for the first time in your life.

DOES THIS MAKE YOU NERVOUS?

GOOD MORNING

I pray you have a great day.

I want to always speak life into you, encouraging you and being your peace.

I want to love on you to the point all you see is me.

I want to create spaces for us to build and grow.

My souls cry out for you, to you.

I look forward to our kiss and next embrace; you have done something to me never done before.

With each day that comes I will show you how much I appreciate and love you because I don't want us to ever go away!

LITTLE THINGS

You're the kind of man that remembers things like the first time we kissed, the first place we went and when things became deeper.
You are intentional with every word, every action and touch.
You pay meticulous attention to me and the details to put a smile on my face.
When you're not physically present, your essence is still nearby.

Doing the unexpected is in your DNA.

You call my line requesting my presence outside, I needed to see your face, kiss your lips and feel your embrace.
You do something to me.
You make me lost for words, my gosh that's so rare.
You notice me, listening, captivated by each word and phrase.
You listen to the beat of my heart drum; it's the little things you do that have me walking on cloud nine, feeling like a high school girl with her first crush.
When you touch me it sends me places, your kiss draws me in as you grab my hips letting me know I'm yours and you're mine.

Your love is on another level, I am star struck.
We are all we see, each other's biggest fans.
No one can step to me to take your place.
You do things to maintain a smile on my face with the
intention to never hurt my heart.
I'm a precious gift in your eyes, this is irrevocable
nothing can come between.

Your love is as rare as a precious stone captivating me
to the core.

The little things you have done have inspired me, moved
me closer to the Son!

I desire to do new things, reevaluate my goals and
dreams.

When you came along you fixed my crown, you see
something greater within me.

You have awakened parts of me that have not existed for
years.

You have reminded me to...

BE BRAVE

BE BOLD

BE ME!

A COUPLE OF...

You came into my life in such a spontaneous way.
You captivate me, having me like a cliff hanger holding
on to your every word.

A couple of interactions, a few smiles, conversations,
texts got me mesmerized thinking of one day you and I
...... oh never mind.

A hug or two, I couldn't really let you know how you
have me.
You called me for lunch, as I approached the door my
heart racing, why?
What have you done to me?
I'm used to being in control of my feelings, but not with
you.

Where is this Man, I call, you say "you seem so
nervous?"
"What do you mean, I don't see you", "keep walking
towards the door, I love to see you walk it does
something to me."

I just smile, I love to hear him speak.
I look around a few times, he walks up from behind
whispers in my ear,
"Come with me, I want to lead you to OUR seat!"

SWEET AUGUST

A day I'll never forget, when you became more than a friend.

You took out time to study every centimeter of me.
You listened to me, my joys and hurts and renewed me.
The call was so sweet, we meet.

I walk into the room candles everywhere, soft music playing.
You welcome me in with roses in both hands.
You greet me with a long passionate kiss as you wrap your hands around my frame.

You wanted to do more, but you have more to come.
My smile became brighter than the sun.
You undressed me and it all began.
With each kiss you subdued me I was like putty within your hands.

You noticed I was shy, ashamed of the journey of childbirth and the residue of stretch marks. You gazed in my eyes and began to kiss each place.
Tears began to fall as you whispered how beautiful I am, scars and all.

So intentional with each word, position, and touch.
My mind is racing, I've never felt this way.

You made it all about me, truly a man of action.
As you wiped away my tears, kissed me slow, my body
began to explode.
As the music played in the background our bodies
connected, with our own unique rhyme our bodies
flowed.

Hour one went by, followed by hour two, it felt so
natural and explosive.
I could not stop the sweet juices from flowing, it made
him go longer and harder.
Hour three, I laid in his arms gazing in his eyes, this man
can't be real.
The way I feel at this moment has me lost for words, I
wanted to show him how much he means to me.

I put the covers over my head and thanked him slow on
my knees, kissing his inner thigh, he's losing his mind.
As he moved, I followed letting him know the emotions
that he has resurrected within me. As time passed, he
took me by the hand and led me into the walk-in shower,
washing me and I him.

Witnessing the look in his eyes was a clear indicator
that he needed me again, and I him. Bending over, water
running across my back he grips the sides of the shower
as his head falls back in sheer ecstasy.

The feeling of my wet mouth on his large erect manhood
felt so invigorating as it hits the back of my throat with
each stroke, causing his knees to become weak, his grip

becoming tighter.

I stop he turns around whispers in my ear "my turn!"
His touch sends chills in places that have been closed
off.
He has awakened love.
Oh, how sweet August has become!

MY WARRIOR & KING

You are so unique and extraordinary; you captivate me
with your words and presence.

Watching you command a room does something to me.

Your protection and provision is something you don't see
often.

You are where I go to hide when the winds of life begin
to blow, when lightning strikes and the thunder rolls.

My warrior you are where I go to slow down, you are my
favorite place, my sacred space.
You are my peace, you help me be still.
You are who I go to for prayer, talk politics or places in
my life that have hurt me and caused me pain.

I can drop my garments with you in full disclosure.
I know you will handle me with care.
Your kiss subdues me at times I feel suspended in air.
What's come over me?

Your love and presence my *King* make me new.
It has rejuvenated me, changed the way I think wanting
to try my hand at love again.
You are my favorite place to go to when I need to let
down my hair.

You challenge me to be better.
You have helped me heal; you have disclosed something so pure and true.

You make love to my mind; the thought of you causes me to climax.
You have touched the essence of my soul.

When we are around one another it's like our souls intertwine and say, "Welcome home."
When we make love, you become *King* of the sheets, taking me on a new journey we both have never traveled.
With each intentional touch it does something to me, with each kiss and embrace, our bodies cry out in ecstasy.
I feel like I have an out of body experience with each climax.

WHAT WILL I DO WITHOUT MY WARRIOR, MY KING?

WILD PINK & WHITE SEPTEMBER

You began my day with our normal morning calls and FaceTime, followed by deep casual conversations and questions.
As usual a smile comes across our faces, followed by "where are you?" "Headed to the church to do some work."

Another FaceTime, looking at his face it causes me to have a series of feelings.

Once again asking my location on my way. Pulling up a black Jeep pulls behind, waving them around, but no movement. Getting out I approach the driver asking if she needs assistance? She quickly informed me she was here for a delivery and could not miss the intended individual.

May I have the name? I quickly asked as there were people inside.
"The last name Florence, let me get the arrangement to confirm the first name."
To my surprise she asks if I can assist her locating Clianda Florence?

My face became as bright as the sun and full of surprise; I am her.
Her next reply "Happy Belated Birthday from someone

who Loves You!"
A beautiful dozen of Wild Pink Roses, accompanied with round green leaves.
Speechless, I text "can you call me?"

Moments later my phone rings, hearing your voice sends chills.
As I attempt to get my question out, I can hear your smile followed by "I told you I do the unexpected. I could have sent them to your home, but I wanted to send them where you are, so everyone can see what captured me ... your beautiful SMILE."

"I also wanted to put everyone on notice, you have a REAL MAN!"

YOUR HANDS

Your touch sends chills through my body.
When you touch the small of my back my body reacts.

I don't know what you're doing to me.
I'm leaving my fragile heart in your hands, please don't break it.
I love how you do whatever you can to put a smile on my face.
I'm beginning to let down my guard, allowing you in.

You do the unexpected!
You pay close attention to me, how my body reacts to you and what I need.

With you, I desire to reach new heights.
I want to reach for the stars, venture down new paths, and dream new dreams.

Baby, at times I'm lost for words when it comes to you.

I trust you to lead the way.

When I close my eyes and you kiss my lips, I yearn for you to touch me and pull me in.
I love how you cover me!

I desire to please you, giving you whatever you need.
The ***essence of my soul*** lay within your hands; I only ask that you handle me with CARE.

CAN I ...

Touch you
Speak to you
Capture the essence of your *Soul*

Suck you nice and slow
Make you feel good, while renewing you
I can see it in your eyes, you want to
Bend me over
Suck on me
Touch me
Slide inside the shower
As you talk in my ear
It's time to release
Can I touch you there?

Thank you
For hearing me
Seeing into me
Heeding & Healing Me
Loving me unconditionally
Covering me like no other
Affording me the space to BE
Not intimidated by my past

Or

What I bring to the table

Providing provision & protection
Ministering to me, the very essence of me
Being my peace
Affording me the opportunity to experience a Real Man
Real Love
The way you study me, your intentionality
The unexpected
Keeping a smile on my face

ASTONISHED

Missing you
Yearning for your touch more than you know
Needing to hear your voice within my inner ear

You make my heart skip a beat,
Speechless
A new smile, a new heart song, a new Cli.

As the water reaches the points of the sea, is as vast as
my love is

I keep wondering what have you done to me?
You hit me with a deep quote
"An awake heart is like a sky that pours light."

Hitting me with

"Thinking of your wet pussy throbbing on my dick,
while I say sweet things in your ear, ensuring you will
always know how special you are to me. The thought
of thrusting my manhood into you so deep I get an arch
in my back. I want your caramel thighs to melt in my
mouth,

wrapping them around my face,
followed by my waist
as our

Love making creates a unique rhythm
only a flow we know.

Communicating to you how much you mean to me,
how much
I Love You."

Damn, you got me speechless and *astonished!*

CUM INTO ME

I want you to release in my mouth; swallow to always have a part of you with me.

It's something different about you; you have awakened and unleashed the inner FREAK within me.

I feel amazing and renewed; the way you command my body to cum is something I never experienced before.

Your voice, your touch, your picture, your care does something........it's hard to find the words; hold on I got to change my underwear.

Just writing these words about you has me riding high looking forward to mounting you, you holding me grinding, while you look into me.

Oh, to hear your voice in my ear "Stand right here, I need to look at you, touch you and gaze into your eyes."

Can I touch you make you make you feel so good?

I know you want me too he drops to his knees, I rub his head, he enters my Sweet Box!

AM I...

Wrong to miss you
To need you
To want you

Greeting me at the door with roses
Sweet smells and kisses
Your smile illuminating the room as soft music plays
Do you know you take my breath away?

In my presence in between my thighs
I'm getting so wet you touch me
On all four as you taste me from behind
The thought sends chills up my spine

If only you were mine and I yours
Sucking your manhood as my tongue does tricks
Can you see it and feel it yet
I'm so wet dripping down my thighs as I pen these sweet
words to you

Do you really understand what you have done to me?
I wonder what I've done to you.
Am I wrong to need you?
Am I wrong to long for you?
Am I wrong to need you to release in me as I need to
on you?

Am I wrong to want to kiss you?
Hold you, talk to you
Am I?

CAN I?

Sit at your feet while soaking up all the knowledge you possess. Lay in your arms and gaze into your eyes.

Can I?
Kiss you slow as your hands glide across my frame. Touch your face; unbutton your pants look into your eyes as we become filled with passion. Place you in my mouth as I suck you slow, as you grow, causing the juices within me to flow.
The desire and need for covering, care, and voice within my inner ear.

Can I?
Sit on it, going up and down as the sweet nectar drips on your thick erect uhhhh. Stand you in a shower as the water hits my back, fills my mouth pleading for you to climax.
Feel your tongue on my body kissing, touching, and suckin

Can you feel it yet?
I sure can, you got me using my hands closing my eyes wishing it were you.

Can I feel you soon?

PIECE OF MY LOVE

I wish I could sit on your lap and gaze into your eyes, going up and down as you pour your heart out.

I want to suck on your manhood to relax you and lay you down so I can rub you down to show you how much I care.

I want to kiss you to transfer the peace within me that you have freely given me.

AS I...

Reflect on your voice, but your eyes reflecting what your soul is truly saying, thinking
I wish I could reach out and touch your lips to feel all that you're holding inside at times I sit and cry.

The essence of me calls for you. I wonder if you can hear anymore. I want to pull you near I need to hear your voice in my inner ear the rhythm of the beat against my ear drum you know the sound that gets me that makes me flow straight to you. How I wish I was in your arms, it's not just sexual your very presence does something magical to me I wish I could stop you from running I wonder do you miss me and does your heart still skip a beat when you think of me?

As I write these words, all I can do is close my eyes and stare to June when you walked in the room sat close to me, star struck wishing I had some Starbucks. Does that line still ring a bell?

Oh well, as I let the water run on me like you use to be ..... I still love you; think of you, I absolutely adore you!

JOY

You don't know how much joy and encouragement you have brought to my life.

You have inspired me to go into the deep, making my own way.

I love you so much more than you know!

GOOD MORNING

I can't get you out my mind, your voice, your touch, your kiss, your words spoken and unspoken. The mutual need we both share the hunger that only we can cure.

Before I thought it was just words but we share an irrevocable bond.

I close my eyes replaying in my mind the last time I was with you, the thought of you vulnerable and anticipating me as I you.

Our feelings run so deep, if only you knew how much you mean to me.

Looking forward to our time, I miss the candles, flowers, and care. I need that, I need you!

THANK YOU

For pouring into me
Seeing me
Reviving me
Restoring me
Encouraging me
Returning passion to me
Healing me at my broken places.

Thank You
For bringing joy inside my tears
Helping me to overcome my fears
Inspiring me to step out on faith
Aiding me to see a bigger brighter world than I thought.

Thank You
For your patience
Serenading me
Showing me the blueprint of how a man should treat a
woman
Correcting me and being open with me
Trusting me with you.

Thank You
For opening up sacred space for me to dwell
For touching my soul
I thank God for you a beautiful creation fashioned for me
showing me real intimacy
My Soul Mate!

IMAGINED

You make me feel like a natural woman
You take me to heights never imagined
With you I feel free, I can be
You love every inch of me.

I feel alive like I can thrive
When I'm in your arms, it's like the great escape, my
safe space I can retreat and " BE" at peace.

You help center and ground me
I am filled with so much joy
The kool-aid smile makes me feel like a kid excited to
see their best friend.

You are my crush,
I'm your biggest fan, jumping, screaming, and waiving
both hands.

You move me to a beat of a drum the sounds, your voice
your touch is next to none
You make me feel,
You make me feel,
You make me feel like I can breathe again
I Love you
Adore you
Admire you!

PICTURE PERFECT

In another life
I would have been honored
to be your wife.
Reality is,
my desires are just a dream.
I still ......
see you and me perfectly
in a frame fading slowly
Picture perfect
you will always be to me!

SUBMERGE

If I could be water gliding across your lower extremity, submerging it with my warm mouth as your head falls back and my ass in the air. Going up and down hearing you softly make sounds causing my sweet inner walls to fill. Patiently waiting for you to lay me down for round after round.

You can no longer take it causing me to stop not wanting your DNA to drop. You take me by my hand telling me how beautiful I am, you instruct me to sit on your face so you can taste my sweet loving. My legs begin to shake I want to return the favor, so we go down route 69. The feeling is explosive. You stop me and say softly I need to see your face.

You lay me down and look into my eyes as your erect manhood glides inside. Know that I will always love you, you mean more to me than you think. You have healed me at my broken places. I can hear you say softly, your husband loves every part of you. I can no longer take it tears coming down my face with each stroke. You kiss me as you go deeper into me.

You tell me to turn around, my ass in the air you spread my cheeks entering in. With each pump my body responds to you, my inner walls wet with earnest expectation. I can no longer take it. I explode, causing you to go deeper. You turn me back over needing to gaze into my eyes you slow down not ready to release.

You have more to say and share with your homie, lover, friend. It's far too much to bear, we embrace one another as you kiss me so slow. I feel you letting go, your love falling like rain into me.

AUTHENTIC LOVE

He softly whispered... You need my manhood in your mouth, to feel it expanding as you arouse me.
You need my manhood to stir your womanhood into excitement. I love how your strength submits to me in femininity and takes every ounce of me I give you and enjoy your body.

I love your curves, your smell and taste. It awakens the man within me that has been emasculated and unappreciated and it gives me a desire to give you more and more of me.

I love how you shed tears of love and joy as you experience orgasm from my touch and penetration. Just like now I can look at your face and tell how moist you are within your sugar walls not because of anticipated sex but over authentic love.